Looking at Countries

JAPAN

Jillian Powell

FRANKLIN WATTS
LONDON·SYDNEY

First published in 2006 by
Franklin Watts
338 Euston Road
London NW1 3BH

Franklin Watts Australia
Hachette Children's Books
Level 17/207 Kent Street
Sydney NSW 2000

ISBN-10: 0 7496 6886 5
ISBN-13: 978 0 7496 6886 0
Dewey classification: 915.2

Series editor: Sarah Peutrill
Art director: Jonathan Hair
Design: Rita Storey
Cover design: Peter Scoulding
Picture research: Diana Morris

Picture credits: Stephan Boness/Panos: 12, 20. Paul Dymond/Lonely Planet Images: 13. Robert Essell NYC/Corbis: 7b. Joson/zefa/Corbis: 26t. Catherine Karnow/Corbis: 11t. Karen Kasmanski/Corbis: 15t. Issei Kato/Corbis: 9. Charles & Josette Lenars/Corbis: 15b. Paul Quale/Panos: 14. Chris Stowers/Panos: 17. Superbild/A1 Pix: front cover, 6, 11b, 25t, 25b, 26b. Superbild/Incolor/A1 Pix: 1, 4, 7t, 8, 10. 16, 18, 19b, 21, 23, 24, 27. Tom Wagner/Saba/Corbis: 22. Michael S. Yamashita/Corbis: 19t. Every attempt has been made to clear copyright. Should there be any inadvertent omission please apply to the publisher for rectification.

A CIP catalogue record for this book is available from the British Library.

Printed in China

Franklin Watts is a division of Hachette Children's Books.

Contents

Where is Japan?

Japan is in Asia. It is made up of four main islands and thousands of smaller islands in the Pacific Ocean.

Japan has no land borders with any other country.

EUROPE

ASIA

— Japan

PACIFIC OCEAN

AFRICA

Japan's capital city, Tokyo, is on the largest island, Honshu. Tokyo has old palaces, temples, shrines and gardens. It also has modern skyscrapers with offices, banks and shops.

Tokyo is a busy, crowded city with streets of tower blocks.

Japan's nearest neighbours across the Sea of Japan are Korea, China and Russia.

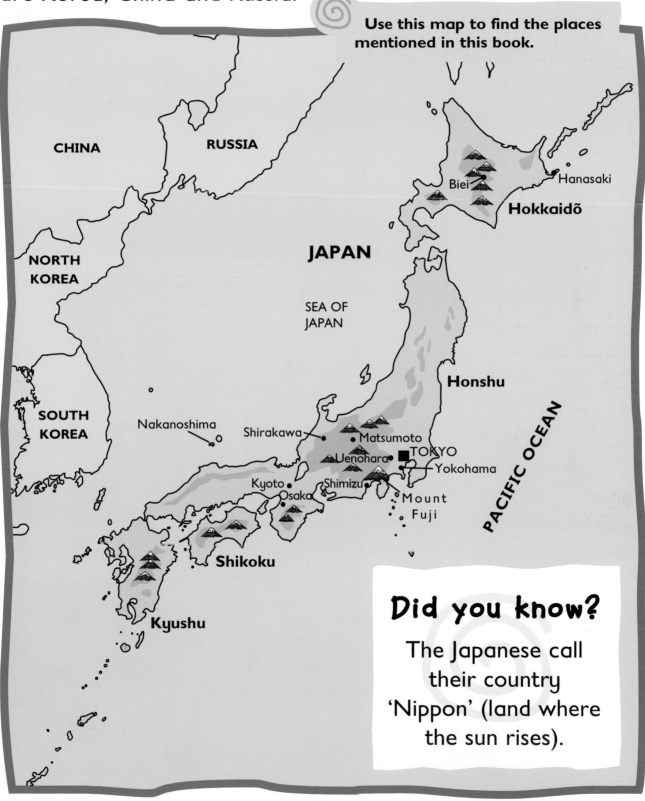

Use this map to find the places mentioned in this book.

CHINA

RUSSIA

Hanasaki

Biei

Hokkaidõ

JAPAN

NORTH KOREA

SEA OF JAPAN

Honshu

SOUTH KOREA

Nakanoshima

Shirakawa

Matsumoto

TOKYO

Uenohara

Yokohama

Kyoto

Shimizu

Osaka

Mount Fuji

PACIFIC OCEAN

Shikoku

Kyushu

Did you know?

The Japanese call their country 'Nippon' (land where the sun rises).

The landscape

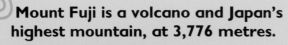

Japan is a land of lakes, rivers, streams and high mountains. Many of the mountains are volcanoes.

Did you know?

Japan has lots of small earthquakes every year.

Mount Fuji is a volcano and Japan's highest mountain, at 3,776 metres.

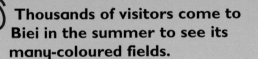
Thousands of visitors come to Biei in the summer to see its many-coloured fields.

Less than one quarter of Japan's land can be used for farming. Most farms are on flat land along the coast and in the river valleys. Farmers grow fruit and vegetables and keep animals such as chickens. Rice is grown in flooded fields called paddies, in valleys and on terraced mountain slopes.

Rice growing on terraces around the port of Shimizu on the east coast of Honshu.

Weather and seasons

There are big differences in the weather in the north and south of Japan. The northern islands have long cold winters and short warm summers. There can be lots of snow and ice in winter, especially in the mountains.

In the south, it is warm all year round. Winters are mild and summers are hot. Most rain falls between June and September.

Did you know?

The Japanese hold parties called *hanami* to welcome cherry blossom in the spring.

Oranges grow in the warmer climate of the south.

This damage was caused by a typhoon that hit the island of Nakanoshima.

From September to November, there can be tropical storms called typhoons. Typhoons can cause lots of damage, and bring in heavy rain and tidal waves from the Pacific Ocean.

Japanese people

The Japanese are proud of their culture and traditions. Respect for others, especially older people and family ancestors, is important to most Japanese. They also believe in working hard.

The main religions in Japan are Buddhism and Shintoism. Most homes have a special place or room where people pray to family ancestors. They also pray at temples or shrines at important times such as a wedding or the birth of a child.

There are over a thousand Shinto shrines and Buddhist temples in Kyoto, which was once Japan's capital city. This is a Buddhist temple.

A monk tidies a Zen garden that is based on Buddhist ideas of calm.

Did you know?

There are special schools where girls can learn how to put on and tie kimonos.

This woman wears a traditional Japanese kimono as she carries out the tea ceremony in Kyoto.

The tea ceremony, *chanoyu*, is a popular Japanese tradition. This is a special way to make tea that was first practised by Buddhist monks and is now taught at tea clubs and schools. People use the ceremony to entertain family and friends, and tourists visiting Japan.

School and home

Home life, family and education are important to most Japanese people.

Japanese children must start school when they are six but many start at three or four years old. The school day starts at 8.30 am and finishes at 4.30 pm. All children wear school uniform and study the same subjects. They learn to read and write Japanese and one other language, often English.

This girl is wearing a typical secondary school uniform.

At the end of each day, children clean and tidy their classrooms before going home.

This family is sharing a meal together at home. They are eating from a pot in the middle of the table.

Many Japanese parents today have only one or two children, but aunts, uncles and grandparents may live with the family. Everyone plays their part in family life. Most families share a meal together in the evening.

Did you know?

About four out of ten Japanese families have pets at home. The most popular pets are dogs, followed by cats and fish.

Country

In the country, many people live on small family farms. They may grow rice and another crop such as apples.

This man is planting out rice seedlings using a small machine.

Grandparents help with the farming as they often live with the family. Children will help after school and in the holidays with jobs such as feeding chickens or pigs.

Did you know?

Bears live in the wild in parts of Japan.

Planting and harvesting are often done by hand although some farmers own small machines or share larger machinery with their neighbours. Many country people are part-time farmers, and do other jobs to bring in more money. Around the coasts, for example, people go fishing, or gather seaweed to eat.

These women are harvesting a tea crop by hand.

It is traditional for Japanese mothers to carry their babies on their backs. In the country they may do this when they are working in the fields.

City

These skyscraper buildings are in Yokohama, an important port city on the island of Honshu.

Four out of five people in Japan live in towns or cities. Most cities are built on the coast. Tokyo, Yokohama and Osaka are the largest cities. The Imperial Palace, the home of the Japanese Emperor, is in Tokyo.

People in Tokyo rush to work. Some are wearing face masks to protect themselves from pollution.

People live busy lives in the cities. Many people have the latest hi-tech goods and go to western-style shops and fast-food restaurants. Japan's cities are crowded with people and traffic and there can be air pollution.

Cities have good public transport systems including buses and underground trains.

Did you know?

'Pushers' squeeze people onto underground trains in Japan during busy times of the day.

Japanese homes

Traditional old houses in Japan are built from wood with paper windows. Inside, they have thick rice-straw mats called *tatami* on the floors. Paper or bamboo screens divide the house into rooms. Some old houses with thatched roofs can still be seen in the mountains.

Did you know?

Japanese people leave their shoes by the door to keep the *tatami* clean inside their homes.

This is a traditional Japanese house with a thatched roof in Shirakawa, a village in a mountain area known as the Japanese Alps.

These low-rise blocks of flats in the port city of Osaka have balconies for outdoor space.

In the cities, most people live in small flats in high-rise blocks. In the suburbs, people live in flats in low-rise blocks or in estates of houses with gardens.

Many people live in estates of houses like these in the suburbs of Uenohara and travel into Tokyo to work.

Food

Fish, vegetables, rice and noodles are all important foods in the Japanese diet. Soya beans are used widely in cooking and sauces. Meat such as chicken and pork is cooked in stews or cut into thin strips and deep fried or stir fried with vegetables.

Sushi is a popular fast food in cities. Western-style fast foods such as burgers are also popular.

This sushi bar is popular with city workers.

This stall on the Ameyoko market street in Tokyo sells fresh fish.

Fresh foods such as fish, seaweed and vegetables are bought from markets or small shops. In towns and cities, people also shop at supermarkets.

At home, many families eat traditional meals, sharing several small dishes of different foods. They sit at low tables and use chopsticks to eat.

Did you know?

The Japanese always place the pointed ends of the chopsticks on a special rest when the chopsticks are not being used.

At work

The main industries in Japan include iron and steel, ships, cars and motorbikes, and electronic goods, such as mobile phones, computers, cameras and televisions. Japanese cars and electronic goods are leading brands sold around the world.

Did you know?

In the past, people in other countries sometimes said that the Japanese worked too much. But in recent years the number of working hours has been brought down in Japan.

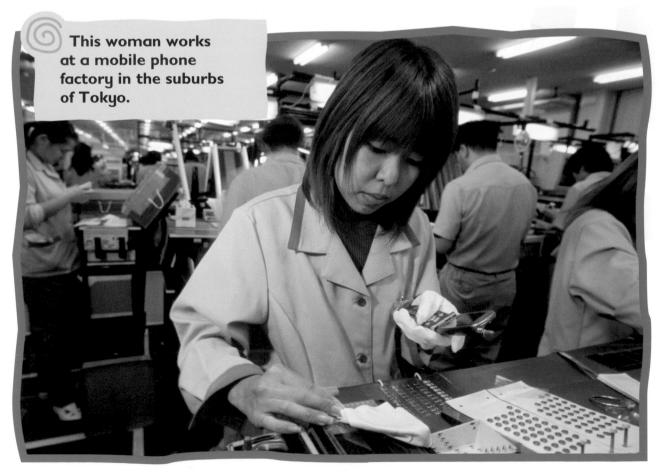

This woman works at a mobile phone factory in the suburbs of Tokyo.

Japanese people also work in banks, shops, schools, hospitals, transport, farming and fishing. Japan is the world's leading fishing nation. It has a large fish-farming industry, with coastal farms producing fish, shellfish and seaweed.

This man is unloading fish at the port of Hanasaki on Hokkaidō.

Having fun

Baseball, football, basketball and golf are all popular sports to play and watch in Japan. Japanese martial arts, such as judo, tae-kwondo and kendo, are taught in schools and clubs. Sumo wrestling is a popular sport for people to watch. Its top stars are well-known in Japan.

Did you know?

Comics (manga) are popular with adults as well as children in Japan.

These children are practising kendo in Matsumoto.

People carry giant paper and bamboo lanterns shaped like heroes for the August Lantern Festival.

Some people enjoy going to the theatre. *Kabuki* is a traditional theatre, which tells stories of Japan's past with actors wearing colourful make-up and costumes. Young people enjoy television, computer games and karaoke.

There are colourful festivals through the year, celebrating special times such as the rice harvest. There are ceremonies, parades of floats and lanterns, fireworks, feasts and dancing.

These children are taking part in a rice-planting festival in Tokyo.

Japan: the facts

• In Japan the Emperor is the head of state and the Prime Minister leads the government. The Japanese parliament is called the Diet. Its members are elected by the Japanese people.

• Japan is divided into 47 different regions, each with its own governor.

The Japanese currency is the yen.

The Japanese flag shows a red circle (a rising sun) on a white background.

Japan's high-speed 'bullet' trains link Tokyo with other major cities.

• Japan has a population of over 127 million people.

• Eleven cities in Japan have populations of over a million people. The largest is the capital, Tokyo. Over 12 million people live in the city and its suburbs.

Did you know?

5th May is a public holiday called 'Children's Day' in Japan. People celebrate the health, growth and happiness of children.

Glossary

Ancestors   family members who died long ago.

Bamboo   a tall plant with hard, hollow stems.

Buddhism   a world religion based on the teachings of Buddha who lived around 563–483 BCE.

Chopsticks   a pair of sticks used for eating.

Culture   the ideas, beliefs and art of a people.

Earthquake   a time when the ground shakes.

Head of state   a person who is the main representative of a country.

Karaoke   singing songs along with a recording of the music.

Kendo   a type of fencing, using bamboo swords.

Kimono   the traditional dress of Japan.

Martial arts   Sports of combat and self-defence. Many come from Asia.

Paddy fields   fields that are flooded with water for growing rice.

Pollution   dirt in the air and ground caused by industry and cars.

Shintoism   a Japanese religion based on the worship of ancestors and nature spirits.

Shrine   a place or building for prayer, used in Shinto and other religions.

Suburbs the area outside a town or city, where people mostly live rather than work.

Sumo a Japanese sport where two people fight without weapons.

Sushi fish served in small pieces with rice and sauces.

Temple a building for prayer in Buddhism, Hinduism and other religions.

Terraced land on slopes that has been cut into steps to make fields.

Tidal waves huge, damaging waves caused by storm winds or earthquakes.

Typhoons tropical storms with very high winds.

Valley low land between hills.

Volcanoes mountains that can throw out hot rock and gases.

Find out more

http://web-japan.org/ kidsweb/say.html
A section of kidsweb Japan for learning to read and write some words in Japanese.

www.ksky.ne.jp/~akihiroh
A website describing the lives of children living in Chichibu, Japan, with information on Japanese homes, games and sports.

http://web-japan.org/kidsweb
A children's website packed with information on life in Japan, with links to schools in Japan.

Note to parents and teachers: Every effort has been made by the Publishers to ensure that these websites are suitable for children, that they are of the highest educational value, and that they contain no inappropriate or offensive material. However, because of the nature of the Internet, it is impossible to guarantee that the contents of these sites will not be altered. We strongly advise that Internet access is supervised by a responsible adult.

Japanese words

Japanese is usually written with symbols called *kanji*. Traditionally, it is written in columns downwards, starting from the right-hand side of the page. Today, Japanese is often written across the page from left to right.

Speak some Japanese!

English	Say ...
Excuse me	su-mi-ma-sen
Goodbye	sa-yo-na-ra
Hello	kon-ni-chi-wa
I don't understand	wa-ka-ri-ma-sen
I understand	wa-ka-ri-mash-ta
No	i-e
Sorry	go-men-na-sai
Thank you	a-ri-ga-to
Yes	hai

Sample *kanji*:

大	Big
小	Small
古	Old
行	Go
知	Know

Some Japanese words used in the English language

Judo, Karate – martial arts
Origami – a paper art
Sushi – a food made from raw fish

Tsunami – a huge sea wave caused by an earthquake under the sea

My map of Japan

Trace this map, colour it in and use the map on page 5 to write the names of all the places.

Index